HAL LEONARD

BASS METHOD BOOK 1

DELUXE BEGINNER EDITION

BY ED FRIEDLAND

PLAYBACK+
...ed • Pitch • Balance • Loop

...o access audio and video visit:
...w.halleonard.com/mylibrary

Enter Code
...978-1001-1555-5547

T0083367

ISBN 978-1-70517-610-8

Visit Hal Leonard Online at
www.halleonard.com

World headquarters, contact:
Hal Leonard
7777 West Bluemound Road
Milwaukee, WI 53213
Email: info@halleonard.com

In Europe, contact:
Hal Leonard Europe Limited
1 Red Place
London, W1K 6PL
Email: info@halleonardeurope.com

In Australia, contact:
Hal Leonard Australia Pty. Ltd.
4 Lentara Court
Cheltenham, Victoria, 3192 Australia
Email: info@halleonard.com.au

Each track is recorded in stereo, with bass panned hard right.
To remove the bass, adjust the balance control on your playback
device or computer.

All instruments performed by Ed Friedland.
Edited by Doug Downing.

THE ELECTRIC BASS

*To access online resources, head over to **www.halleonard.com/mylibrary** and input the code found on page 1!*

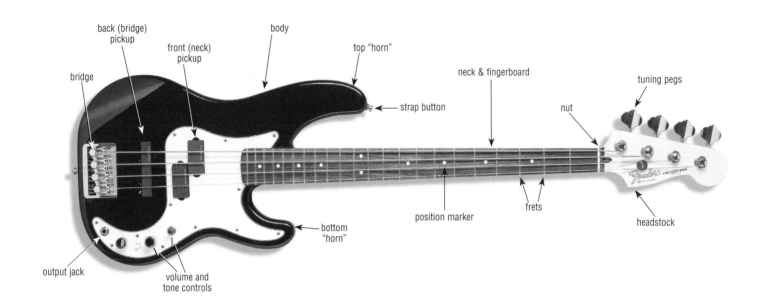

THE BASS AMP

To hear yourself clearly, it is necessary to play an electric bass through an amplifier. Though there are many different sizes, a simple, self-contained unit ("combo") will work fine. Use a patch cord, or cable, to connect from the output of the bass to the input of the amp. Make sure the amp's volume knob is turned off, or all the way counterclockwise. The tone controls should be set "flat," or at 12 o'clock. Turn on the power, and slowly adjust the volume to an appropriate level. Be careful; too much volume could blow out the speaker!

TUNING

TUNING TO THE AUDIO

To tune your bass, adjust the tuning pegs. Tightening a peg will raise the pitch of a string, loosening a peg will lower it.

On Track 1, each string is played four times. The first string you'll hear is the G (1st) string. Check your string with the track; if it sounds lower than the recording, tighten the tuning peg until you get closer to the pitch. If your string is higher, then loosen the peg. Once the G string is in tune, repeat this process with the D, A, and E strings (2, 3, and 4).

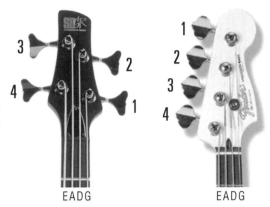

EADG   EADG

USING AN ELECTRONIC TUNER

Electronic tuners have become very affordable, so it's a good idea to have one. There are generally two types available: a "bass" (or "guitar") tuner, which will only read the open strings of your instrument, or a "chromatic" tuner, which will read any pitch. Either will do the job. Plug your bass into the input of the tuner and play your open G string. The tuner will read the pitch and tell you if the string is sharp (too high) or flat (too low). Adjust the tuning peg until the tuner indicates you are in tune. Repeat the process with the D, A, and E strings.

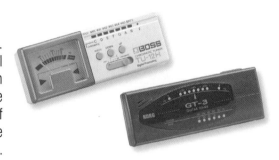

TUNING TO A KEYBOARD

Use the appropriate key on a piano/keyboard to check your open strings.

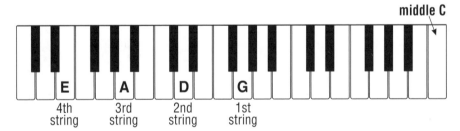

RELATIVE TUNING

Here's another way to tune your bass. It is less accurate, as it assumes that your starting string is in tune—and it is harder for the ear to hear the low pitch of the bass as well as a tuner can—but this method works when there are no other alternatives. It's also a good way to check your tuning.

- Start with your open G string. If there is an accurate G available, use it; otherwise, assume the G string is tuned to the correct pitch.
- Play the D string at the 5th fret, and see if that note matches the open G. Tune the D string up or down until the two notes match.
- Play the A string at the 5th fret; compare it to the open D. Tune the A string up or down until the two notes match.
- Play the E string at the 5th fret; compare it to the open A. Tune the E string up or down until the two notes match.

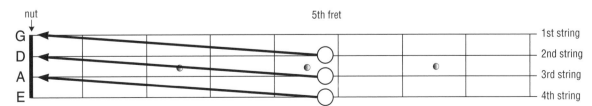

This is called *relative tuning* because the strings are tuned relative to one another.

PLAYING POSITIONS ▶

STANDING

- Buy a comfortable strap between 2½ and 3 inches wide. Leather or woven cotton are good choices. A padded, stretchy neoprene strap will help absorb the weight of the instrument.

- Adjust the strap so that both hands can be comfortable on the bass. With your left arm at your side, bend the elbow, bringing your forearm up. This is your optimal position for the left hand.

- Hold your right arm straight out in front of you at shoulder height, and let the hand hang down naturally. Bend your elbow, and bring your arm in towards your body. That is the optimal position for your right hand.

- Be sure to avoid any extreme bends in either wrist.

TIP: Run the cable under your strap to avoid pulling it out of the jack while standing.

SITTING

- It's best to use a strap while sitting to keep the instrument at the proper height.

- Without a strap, rest the bass on your right leg. It may help to use a small footstool under your right foot.

- Keep your left arm off your leg.

- Angle the neck slightly away from the body.

MUSICAL SYMBOLS

Music consists of two basic elements: **rhythm** and **pitch**. Pitch is notated using a set of lines (and spaces) called a staff. The higher a note appears on a staff, the higher its pitch; the lower a note appears, the lower its pitch. At the beginning of the staff is a clef sign. Bass music is written in the bass clef or "F clef."

The two dots in the clef sign surround the line on which the pitch "F" is written; hence the term "F clef."

The musical alphabet uses the letters **A**, **B**, **C**, **D**, **E**, **F**, and **G**. After G, the sequence repeats starting with A. In bass clef, the notes written on the **lines** of the staff are G–B–D–F–A. You can remember this sequence as "Good Boys Do Fine Always." The notes on the **spaces** are A–C–E–G. "All Cows Eat Grass" may help you remember this.

Rhythm, the other basic element of music, is notated using **measures** (also known as "bars"), which contain a set number of beats (the pulse of the music). Each measure is separated from the next by a **bar line**. A double bar line is used to show the end of a section of music. The final bar line is used to show the end of a piece of music.

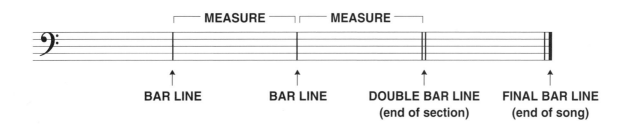

The number of beats in each measure is indicated by the **time signature**, which appears at the start of a piece after the clef sign. The time signature looks like a fraction. The top number tells us how many beats there are in a bar, and the bottom number tells us what type of note is to be counted. Most of the examples in this book will be in 4/4 time.

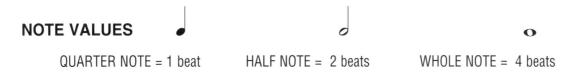

In the first part of this book, you will see three different kinds of note values. They are:

NOTE VALUES

QUARTER NOTE = 1 beat   HALF NOTE = 2 beats   WHOLE NOTE = 4 beats

RIGHT-HAND TECHNIQUE

FINGERSTYLE

The most common approach for playing electric bass is fingerstyle—i.e., using the index (i) and middle (m) fingers of the right hand to play the strings. The fingers give you a warm, full sound that can be controlled easily by developing touch sensitivity.

- Let your fingers hang comfortably, straight over the strings; don't curl them.
- Start by resting the tip of the thumb gently on the pickup.
- Using the fleshy pad of your finger, place it on top of the string.

E STRING

Gently push down and across the top of the E string, letting your finger come to rest against the pad of the thumb. Alternate strokes between the index and middle fingers. Repeat this until you feel comfortable. Play lightly; too much force will give you a distorted sound.

Fingers: i   m   i   m

right-hand position

A STRING

Move your finger to the A string. Push down and across the string, letting your finger come to rest against the E string at the end of the stroke. Alternate fingers; repeat several times.

Fingers: i   m   i   m

end of fingerstroke

D STRING

Drop your thumb to the E string. Move your finger to the D string, push down and across, letting your finger come to rest against the A string. Alternate fingers and repeat.

Fingers: i   m   i   m

muting the E string

G STRING

Drop your thumb onto the A string, and make it lean against the E string. This mutes both strings to prevent unwanted ringing. Put your finger on the G string. Push down and across the string, letting your finger come to rest against the D string. Alternate fingers and repeat.

Fingers: i   m   i   m

TIP: As you alternate fingers, place each finger down for the next stroke just slightly ahead of time, to mute the previous note. This will give you a more controlled bass sound.

muting the E and A strings

PICK STYLE

Pick style produces a clear, distinct sound, and is a very popular technique for playing rock bass. While most bassists tend to use their fingers, pick style is a good skill to have.

The thickness of the pick will affect the tone: A thin pick may be too floppy to produce a strong tone; a heavy pick may not be flexible enough. See what gauge feels right to you.

- Curl your index finger and place the pick on it, letting just the tip stick out.
- Place your thumb over the top of the pick, holding it securely—but not too tightly.
- Make sure the pick is flat against the string; don't use the edge of the pick.
- Rest your pinky against the face of the bass, or on the lower edge of the pickup.

The pick can be used to play **downstrokes** (⊓) and **upstrokes** (∨). The downstroke has a strong attack and works well for hard rock. Play the previous examples again, this time with a pick, using downstrokes (⊓). Use a light wrist motion with a little bit of forearm movement.

Downstrokes:

TIP: To get a full sound from each string, make sure the pick connects fully; let the pick "travel through" and come to rest against the next string after the stroke. Be careful, however, not to play too hard (especially on strings D and G); overplaying can make the string "flap out," producing a weak tone.

> **NOTE**: While you will eventually develop a preference, it's important to play both fingerstyle and pick style to be a well-rounded bassist. Readers are encouraged to learn fingerstyle first—as it presents many unique challenges to the beginning player—and then, at a later time, to try pick style. Any example can be played either fingerstyle or with a pick.

LEFT-HAND TECHNIQUE

Now it's time to start using the left hand. The fingers are numbered 1 through 4 as shown.

1-2-4 FINGERING SYSTEM

The 1-2-4 fingering system allows us to keep the hand relaxed and comfortable, particularly when playing in the lower regions of the bass where the frets are farther apart. Start with the pad of your thumb in the middle of the neck; make sure it doesn't stick up over the top. The thumb is positioned between the first and second fingers.

- Place your first finger directly behind the 1st fret of the E string, pressing down lightly.
- Place your second finger on the 2nd fret.
- Place your fourth finger on the 3rd fret.

1st position

Notice that we have access to three frets—this is called a **position**. We'll study three playing positions in this book: 1st position (with the index finger at the 1st fret), 2nd position (with the index at the 2nd fret), and 3rd position (index at the 3rd fret).

TIP: Keep your left hand relaxed when you play. Never forcibly stretch your hand or hold a position that feels strained.

2nd position

3rd position

OPEN-STRING EXERCISES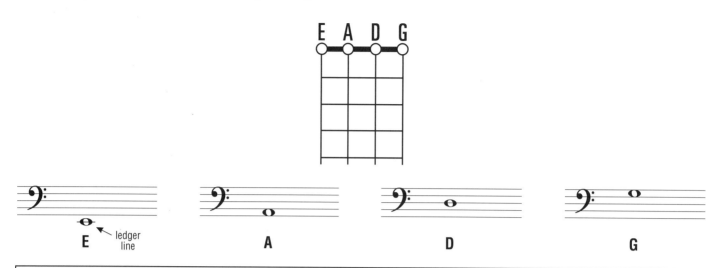

The following exercises are played on the open strings and will help you with basic rhythms, fingerstyle technique, and crossing the strings. Here are the notes for the open strings as written on the staff.

The open E string is written on an added line below the staff, called a **ledger line**.

Each exercise below is played on a single string. Count the rhythms out loud at first, and then play them. As you play, concentrate on alternating between index (i) and middle (m) fingers, as shown.

When playing fingerstyle, the most important thing to remember is to alternate fingers. Once you get used to it, this technique allows you to play notes quickly and easily. You may begin your alteration with either finger—index or middle. Try playing the above exercises again, beginning with "m" instead of "i."

Now let's try playing on more than one string. These exercises move *up* the open strings. Continue to alternate fingers as you move up from one string to the next. Remember to let your fingers "travel through" on each stroke.

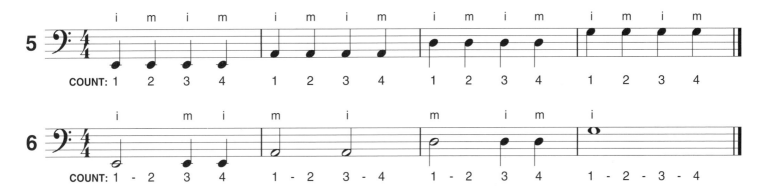

THE RAKE

When moving *down* a string, use the same finger to play both strings—this is called the **rake technique**.

The idea is to use as little effort as possible to get from one string to the next. The rake actually helps keep your right hand relaxed as you move down to the lower string.

Try these exercises moving down the open strings. (Use your left hand to mute the higher open strings.)

This example mixes ascending and descending motion through the strings. It starts on "m," but you could also switch and begin with "i." Remember: When crossing to a higher string, alternate fingers; when crossing to a lower string, use the same finger (the "rake technique") on both strings.

NOTES ON THE E STRING

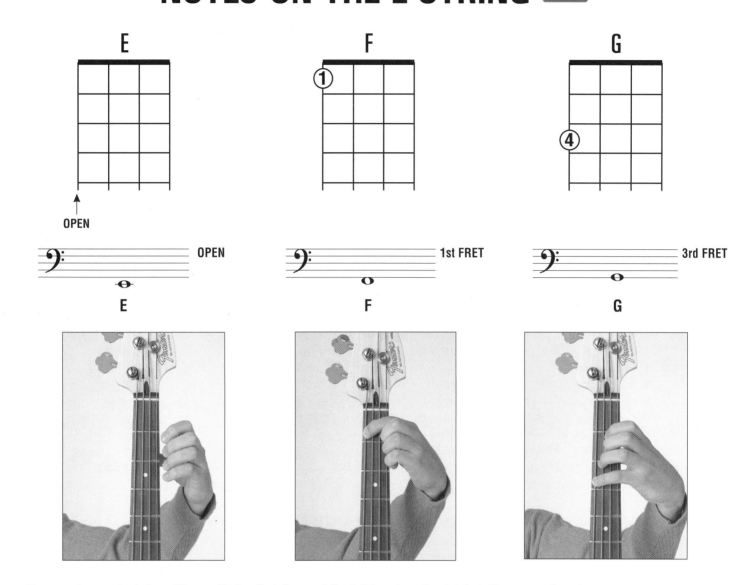

These notes are in **1st position**, with the first finger of the left hand on the 1st fret. Here are a few tips:

- Place your finger directly behind (not on top of) the fret.
- Experiment with different amounts of pressure; it takes less than you think.
- Keep each note ringing until you're ready to play your next note.

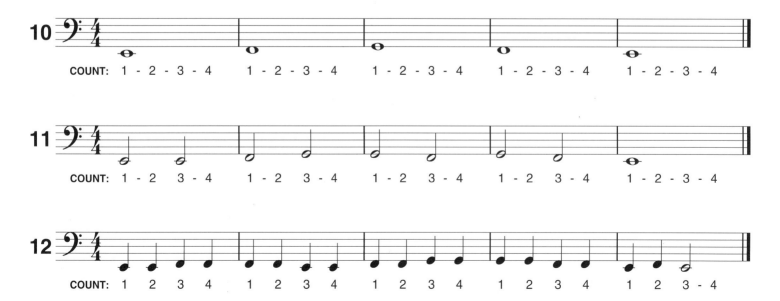

Say the names of the notes out loud while you play, like "E... F... G... F... (etc.)". Remember to alternate i and m fingers in the right hand as you play.

COUNT: 1   2   3   4   1   2   3 - 4   1   2   3   4   1   2   3   4   1 - 2 - 3 - 4

This example skips a space when going from E to G.

COUNT: 1 - 2   3 - 4   1 - 2   3   4   1 - 2   3   4   1   2   3 - 4

Practice keeping the count going on your own.

COUNT: 1 - 2   3 - 4

This next example is 8 measures long. When you reach the end of the first line, continue on to the second line without a pause. The count-off for the track is two measures long: "1... 2... 1, 2, 3, 4..."

LITTLE ROCK

COUNT: 1   2 - 3   4

KINDA FOLKY

MORE NOTES ON THE E STRING

These notes are shown in **2nd position**, with the first finger of the left hand on the 2nd fret.

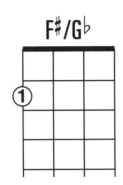

F#/G♭

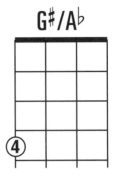

G#/A♭

2nd FRET

F#   G♭

4th FRET

G#   A♭

Why does each note above have two different names? Read on…

So far, the notes you have learned have all been **natural notes**—they have a letter name, and that's all. Notes that occur in between natural notes have names with sharps (♯) or flats (♭) next to them.

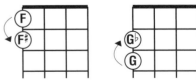

- When you go up one fret from a natural note, its name becomes **sharp** (♯). For example: Play 1st fret F, then move up to the 2nd fret. That note is called F-sharp (F♯).

- When you move down one fret from a natural note, the name becomes **flat** (♭). For example: Play 3rd fret G, then slide down to the 2nd fret. That note is now called G-flat (G♭).

You just noticed that the 2nd fret on the E string has two different names: When you move up from F, we call it F♯; when you move down from G, we call it G♭. That is called an **enharmonic equivalent**.

In written music, a sharp (♯) or flat (♭) placed in front of a note affects every note on the same line or space in that measure. It is automatically cancelled out in the next measure.

18

LOOKIN' SHARP

19

A **natural sign** (♮) cancels a previous sharp or flat. In this example, the G natural is played with the second finger.

20

In the above example, the natural sign "cancels" a sharp from the previous measure. Though not strictly necessary, this helps to avoid any confusion over the intended pitch. This is known as a **courtesy accidental.**

THE SHIFT

In order to play *all* the notes on the E string comfortably, you need to learn how to shift from 1st position to 2nd position. You can shift on any finger: Play the first note, then lighten up on the pressure and slide your hand up or down one fret. Try the following examples, each of which shifts using a different finger.

21

22

23

NOTES ON THE A STRING

A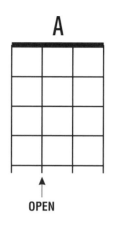

B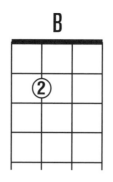

C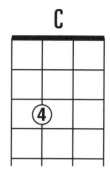

OPEN

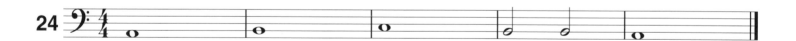
OPEN — A

2nd FRET — B

3rd FRET — C

These notes are in 1st postion. Remember to say the note names out loud as you play.

24

25

26

Practice slowly, to get the notes securely under your fingers. When you feel comfortable with an example, gradually increase the speed.

YOU GO, SLAV

REPEAT SIGN

When a section of music needs to be repeated, a **repeat sign** (:‖) is used. When you reach the repeat sign, go back to the beginning and play the section again, ending at the last measure.

ONE MORE TIME

The next group of exercises will use notes on the E and A strings. Go back and review the E string notes if you need to. Use the rake technique—marked with an asterisk (∗)—when crossing from the A string down to the E string.

This exercise adds F♯ in measure 6. Use the fingering shown. Take the repeat.

CATTLE CROSSING

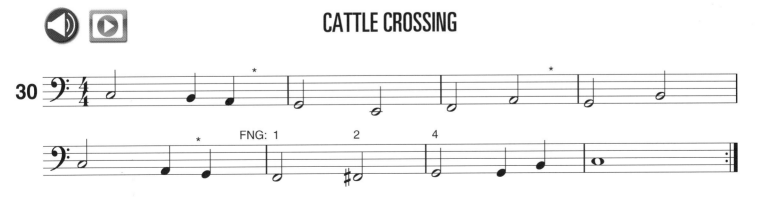

MORE NOTES ON THE A STRING

Just like the E string, the A string has notes that occur in between the natural notes.

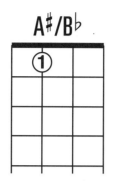

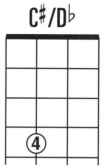

A#/B♭ is in 1st position

C#/D♭ is in 2nd position

This example uses A# with the first finger. It is in 1st position.

This example is also 1st position; it uses B♭ with the first finger.

This example is in 2nd position (make sure your first finger is on the 2nd fret).

THE FINGER ROLL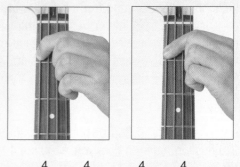

A special technique for the left hand is the **finger roll.** This helps you when playing notes on adjacent strings located at the same fret. The goal is to cross smoothly from one string to the next. To do this when moving from a lower to a higher string, play the note on the lower string using the tip of the finger (with the small knuckle slightly bent); then, flatten the knuckle and roll your finger across, playing the note on the higher string with the pad of the finger.

This example thoroughly works the finger roll on all fingers. Observe the position shifts indicated.

ROLL IT

This 2nd position exercise has several string crossings (and uses A♭ on the way down from open A). In measures 3 and 4, there are finger rolls between G and C.

ROLLY

THE 12-BAR BLUES

Let's play a longer song form, a **12-bar blues**. This is a common progression in rock, jazz, blues, and many other styles of music. The bass line corresponds directly to **chords** that a guitarist or pianist plays. They will be written above each measure so that your teacher or a friend can play along with you. If you examine the bass line, you will see that when the chord symbol says E7, the bass starts the measure with an E; when the chord changes to A7, the bass plays A; etc. You are playing the *root* of the chord, a very important aspect of functional bass playing.

This line is mostly in 2nd position, with an occasional shift down to 1st position. There are only a few fingerings and shift indications written in to help you. Measure 4 has a pattern called a **triad**—three notes that "spell out" the contents of a chord.

12-BAR BLUES

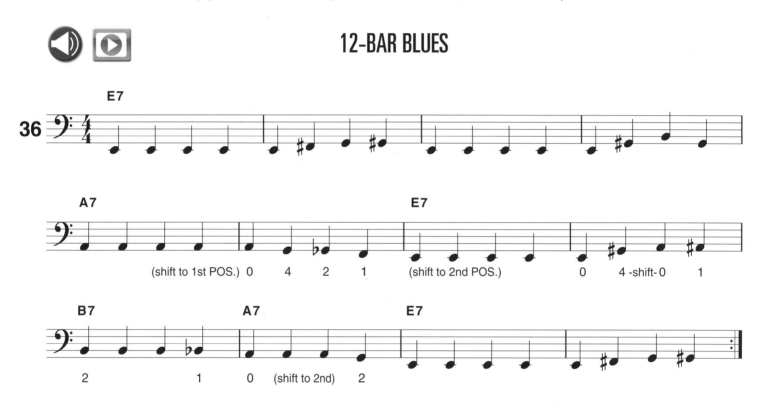

Here is another 12-bar blues. This one changes chords in the 2nd and the 12th measures, a common variation in blues form.

A LITTLE HEAVY

NOTES ON THE D STRING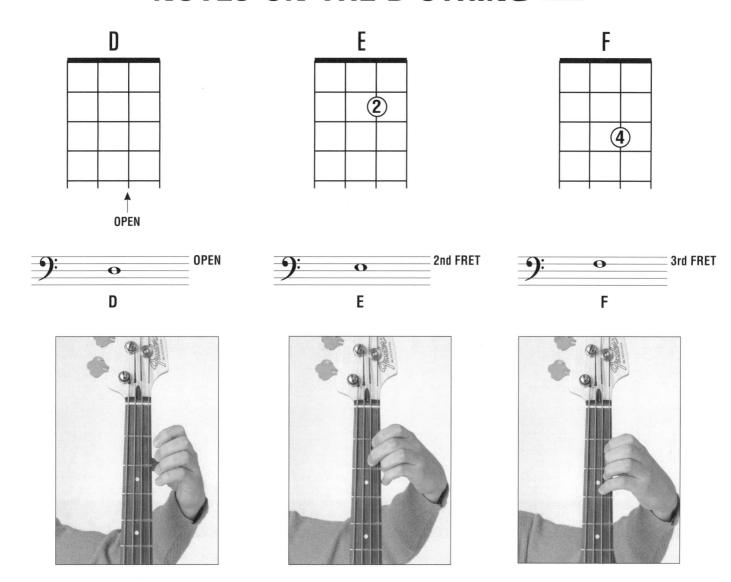

When playing on the D string, remember to drop your right-hand thumb to the E string to keep it muted. Pull straight across with the finger and into the A string. Pick style players: concentrate on your pick accuracy and touch. Don't play the D string too hard.

PRIVATE EYE

This 1st position example crosses the A and D strings. The chord names are included so others can play along. You are playing the root when each chord changes. The symbol "Dm" is for a D minor chord. **Minor chords** sound dark while **major chords** (without the "m") sound happy and bright. Listen for the difference. Watch out for the finger roll in the last measure.

MINOR LEAGUE

1ST and 2ND ENDINGS

The next song has a **1st** and **2nd ending** (indicated with brackets and the numbers "1" and "2"). Play through the 1st ending like a standard repeat sign, and go back to the beginning. The second time through, skip the entire 1st ending and go directly to the 2nd ending section.

This example starts and ends on D; it outlines the sound of the **key** of D. D is the **tonic** or "home base" of the piece. Notice how the bass is not always playing the root when the chords change. You can play other notes that belong to the chord. (This will be explained in depth in Book 2.)

D-LITE

MORE NOTES ON THE D STRING

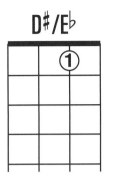 D#/E♭

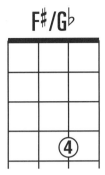 F#/G♭

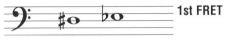 1st FRET

D# E♭

 4th FRET

F# G♭

D#/E♭ is in 1st position

F#/G♭ is in 2nd position

43

Remember to start in 2nd position.

44

This example shifts between 1st and 2nd position.

45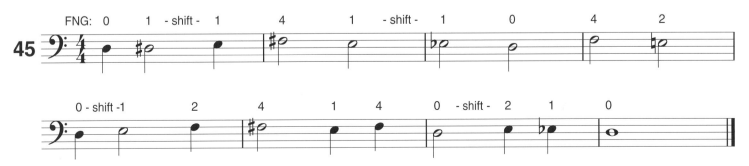

THREE-STRING REVIEW

Here are all the notes you have learned so far. Review each note and solidify your understanding of where it is played on the fingerboard and how it is written on the staff.

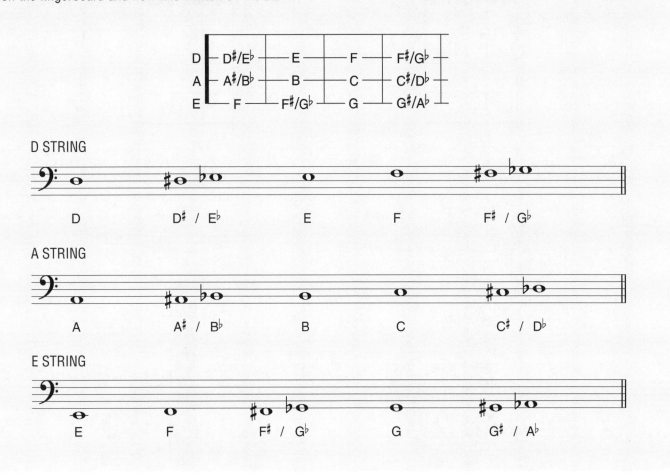

This 2nd position example crosses the three strings you've learned so far. Make sure to follow the 1st and 2nd endings.

CROSSIN' THREE

THE OCTAVE

It's time to look at a musical pattern that is very common in bass playing, the "octave." An **octave** is the same note up or down eight letters in the musical alphabet. For instance, the last two notes in the previous example were both E, but one was high, and one was low—that is an octave.

```
                      octave
                  ┌─────────────┐
musical alphabet - E  F  G  A  B  C  D  E
                  1  2  3  4  5  6  7  8
```

The octave follows a physical pattern on the fingerboard. From any note on the E (or A) string, move up 2 frets, and across 2 strings. This pattern is consistent throughout the fingerboard.

Fingering an octave (without an open string) requires you to play the low note with the first finger, and the high note with the fourth finger.

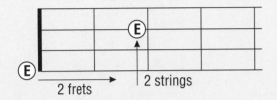

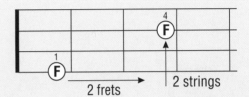

For fingerstyle, use your index finger (i) for the low note of an octave and your middle finger (m) for the higher note.

This example uses the octave shape. For fingerstyle, make sure to drop the right thumb onto the E string when making the jump across to play the D string. This example also shifts up with the first finger to 2nd position. Shifting around the octave shape is a very common practice in bass playing.

OCTA GONE

NOTES ON THE G STRING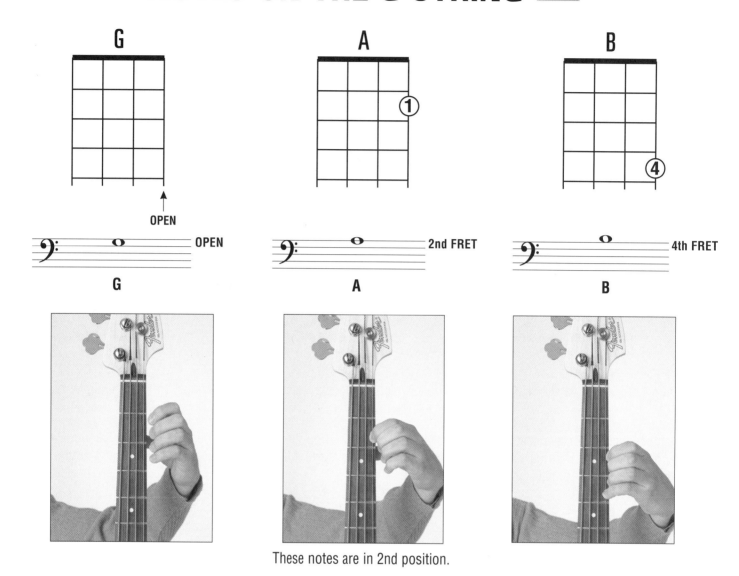

These notes are in 2nd position.

When playing on the G string, make sure your right thumb drops to the A string (muting the bottom two open strings).

This example is in 2nd position and crosses over to the D string. Fingerings are written where necessary.

GEE WHIZ

Now we cross over to the A string. There is a small shift with the 1st finger (indicated simply with "-") from E to E♭ and back.

ALL RIGHT

Now you'll play across all four strings using only the natural notes. Start in 2nd position, and watch for the shifts.

MORE NOTES ON THE G STRING

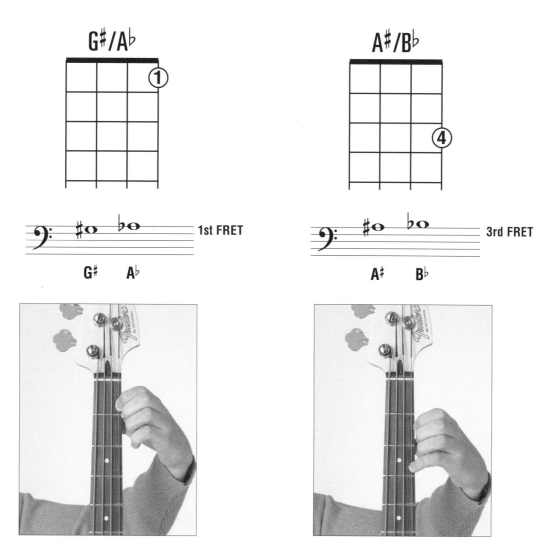

1st FRET

G#   A♭

3rd FRET

A#   B♭

G#/A♭ and A#/B♭ are in 1st position.

This one begins in 2nd position, and then shifts between 1st and 2nd (shifts are indicated with a dash "-").

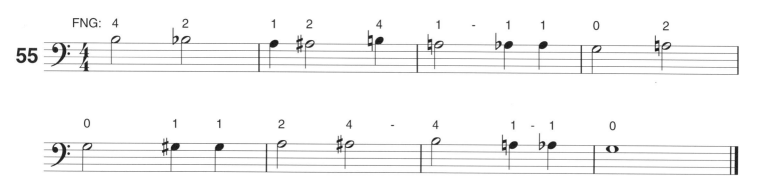

Time for more practice playing across all four strings. This is mostly 2nd position, with one note in 1st position.

ALL FOUR ONE

This one is in 1st position, and uses F as the tonic. There is one shift to 2nd position; fingerings are indicated.

F/X

G major is the tonic. Start in 1st position, but shift in the 6th measure. Use the open D string to move to 2nd position.

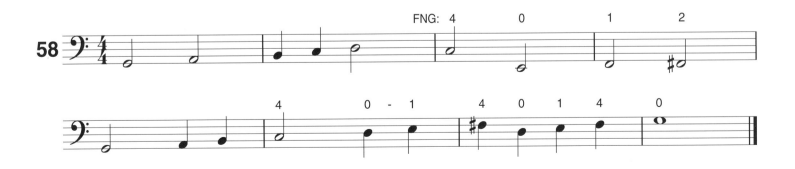

MORE OCTAVES

Playing across all four strings, there are more octave shapes available. Here are the new octaves you can play between the A and G strings. Remember that A♯ and B♭ are enharmonic equivalents.

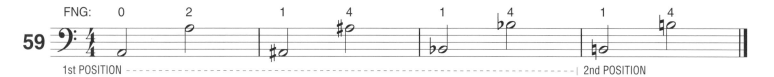

Now let's use all the octaves you've learned so far. The shifts are indicated with a dash "–".

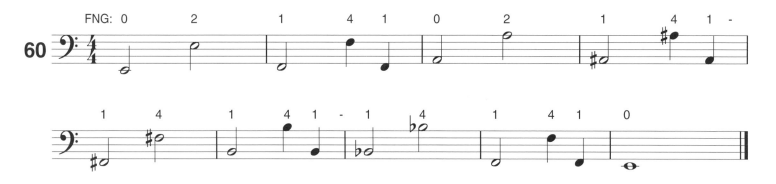

> Because both notes of an octave are the same letter, they can both be considered the root of a chord. On an E chord, for example, both low and high E are the root. Understanding this concept will help you to create your own bass lines.

This 12-bar blues uses the octave on each chord for the bass line. The chords are "seventh chords" (E7, A7, and B7). They are a different type of chord than you've seen, but for now the important thing is to play the root (E, A, and B).

Begin in 1st position; for the B7 chord, shift up to 2nd position. Remember, when playing octaves fingerstyle, the lower note of the octave can be muted with the thumb as you move up to play the higher note on the A or D string. As a general rule, use your middle finger (m) when jumping to the higher note, and your index finger (i) when jumping back down to the low octave.

OCTAVE BLUES

TIES

A **tie** connects two notes of the same pitch. It is used to extend the note value across a bar line, or sometimes within a measure. Play the first note, and hold it for the combined value of both notes.

COUNT: 1 - 2 3 - 4 - 1 2 3 - 4 - 1 - 2 3 4 - 1 - 2 - 3 - 4

3 BEATS   4 BEATS   5 BEATS

62

COUNT: 3 - 4 - 1   4 - 1

3 - 4 - 1 - 2   4 - 1 - 2

In this example, some of the chords change on the first beat of a tie. The key is B minor; notice the darker quality of the song.

TAIWAN ON

63
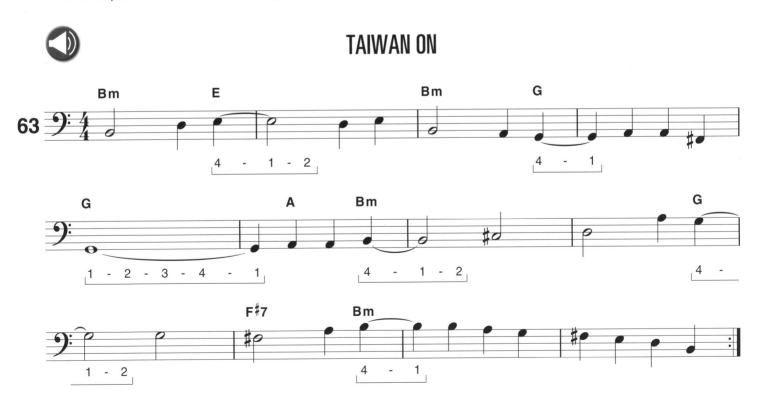

Bm   E   Bm   G

4 - 1 - 2   4 - 1

G   A   Bm   G

1 - 2 - 3 - 4 - 1   4 - 1 - 2   4 -

F#7   Bm

1 - 2   4 - 1

3/4 TIME & THE DOTTED HALF NOTE

3/4 time has three beats per measure, and the quarter note receives one count.

$\dfrac{3}{4}$ → three beats per measure

→ a quarter note (♩) gets one beat

A **dot** after a note extends the note's duration by one-half. A **dotted half note** equals 3 beats.

This has a country waltz feel, and the tonic is C.

THREE'S A CROWD

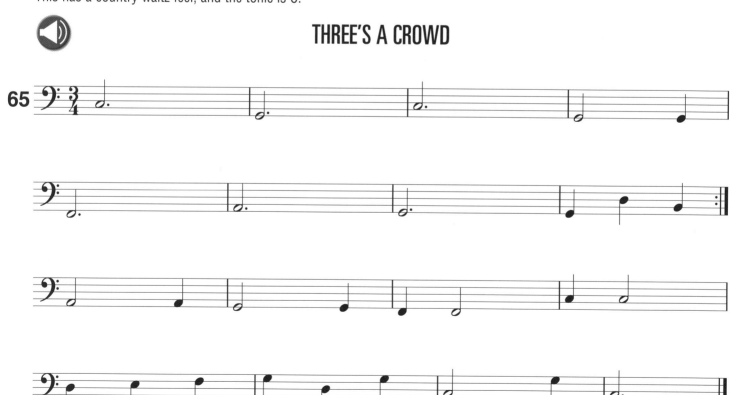

This example is a gospel-flavored tune. The tonic is F.

TELL IT

This piece changes time signatures from 3/4 to 4/4. Count your way through—it's easier than it looks, and it's fun. (Hint: Keep your foot tapping on every quarter note!)

CHANGIN' TIMES

RESTS

Rests are spaces, or silences, in the music, and have specific durations just like notes. In fact, for every note value, there is a corresponding rest of equal value.

It's important to make sure your notes are not still ringing during a rest. Mute the string with your right or left hand, whichever is most convenient.

Although the count is written out only for the first line, keep counting on your own for lines 2–4. Make sure to hold the quarter notes for their full note value.

ROCK 'N' REST

*N.C. = No chord

D.C. al FINE

The marking **D.C. al Fine** is short for "Da Capo al Fine," an Italian phrase meaning, "From the beginning until the end." When you see this marking in a piece of music, go back to the beginning (or "head") of the piece and resume playing until you reach the Fine marking (the "end"), and then stop.

This piece has a jazz-waltz feel. Count through the rests and ties. Note that the root is not always played on each chord.

THREE PLAY

This time, take the D.C. and play the 1st ending back to the beginning; the Fine is the 2nd ending.

EIGHTH NOTES

When you divide a quarter note in half, you get two **eighth notes**. Eighth notes are written separately with flags, or in groups of two or more with beams.

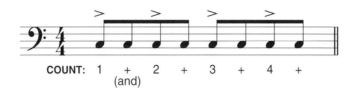

EIGHTH NOTES

In 4/4 and 3/4 time, there are two eighth notes per beat. To count eighth notes, we use the word "and," like this: "1 & 2 & 3 & 4 &." The numbers are called **downbeats**, and the "ands" are called **upbeats**.

For fingerstyle playing, continue alternating index and middle fingers when playing eighth notes. For pick style playing, alternate downstrokes with upstrokes. Use downstrokes (⊓) on the downbeats and upstrokes (∨) on the upbeats.

Play the following exercise slowly at first. Count aloud, tapping your foot on the downbeats. Keep the count going for yourself on the 2nd and 3rd lines. Then try it again, reversing the fingerings (start with "m").

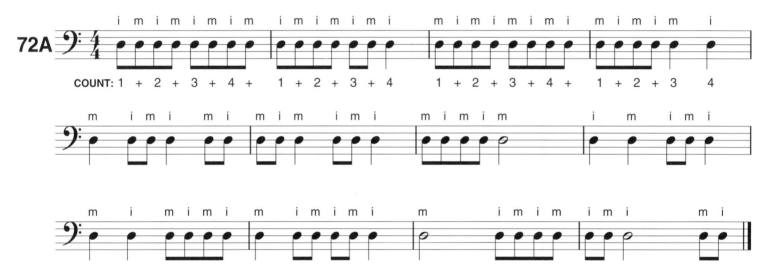

Here's the same exercise played pick style.

For additional practice, try playing each measure individually in a repetitive loop (you'll need to adjust the right-hand fingerings if playing fingerstyle). Add one measure at a time, and eventually play through the entire exercise.

34

This tune combines eighth notes with moving lines. Practice keeping the eye moving ahead fast enough to follow the notes. Make sure to count through the rests.

MOVIN' 8'S

This is in 1st position. F is the tonic or key. Watch for the finger roll with the fourth finger in the last measure.

Notice the use of a consistent idea here; it contributes to a solid bass line. Repetition in the bass part gives a song a feeling of stability and a sense of character.

EIGHT BALL

EIGHTH RESTS

An **eighth rest** takes up the same amount of space as an eighth note. Eighth rests can occur on a downbeat or an upbeat.

Play this example slowly. Tap your foot on the downbeats, and keep counting out loud through the second line. Practice each measure of this exercise separately until you get comfortable with the feel of it, then string them all together. Fingerstyle, continue to alternate index and middle fingers. Pickstyle, keep downstrokes on downbeats and upstrokes on upbeats.

This example uses a two-measure rhythmic pattern to create a consistent feel. There is a slight variation in measure 7.

ROK GRUV

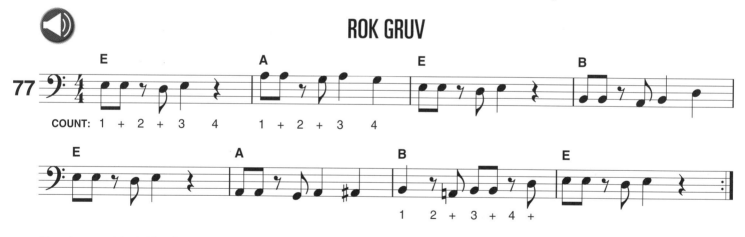

Here is a cool feel. The "and" of beat 2 gets emphasized.

BOP BOP

36

D.C. al CODA

Like "D.C. al Fine," this marking tells you to return to the beginning of the piece. But "al Coda" indicates that you jump to the coda or "tail" section when you reach the appropriate marking. Here is an example with numbered instructions.

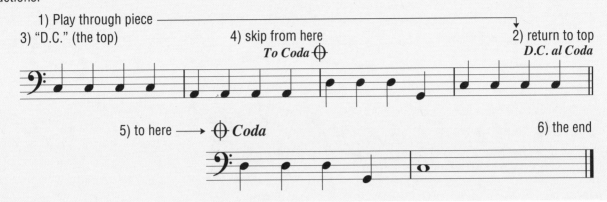

Pay attention to the form of this piece: 1) Take the repeat sign to the top, 2) play through to the second half of the song, 3) follow the D.C. al Coda back to the top, and, 4) at the coda sign, skip to the bottom of the page and play the coda measure.

CODA PENDANT

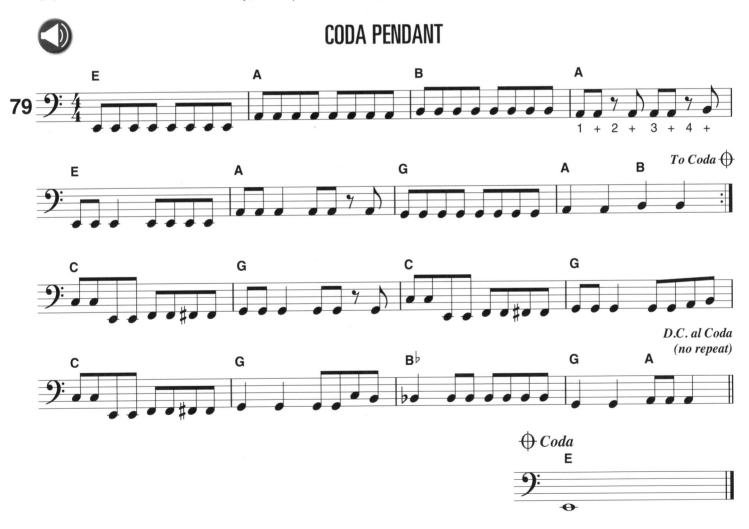

Staying on the root and "pumping out" eighth notes is a classic approach in rock bass playing. Pick style players may want to try the above song again, using all downstrokes (⊓). This option will give you a heavier sound than alternate picking (downstrokes and upstrokes) and is useful for some songs and styles.

The form of this piece is the same as the previous example, but now the first half of the song is called the A section, and the second half, the B section. These **rehearsal letters** make it easier to keep your place in longer songs and are a handy reference point when talking to other musicians.

DEE DEE

This 3/4 example uses ties within the measure.

USING A METRONOME

An important aspect of bass playing is keeping a steady tempo. A **metronome** will help you do this. Use an electronic or battery-powered model. First, learn an exercise slowly, and make sure you can play it correctly. Then, use a metronome to develop your tempo.

- Set your metronome to a slow tempo—50 beats per minute (bpm), for example.
- Let the click become the quarter-note pulse. Count along with it, "1, 2, 3..."
- Look at the exercise without the bass, and practice reading along with the click (e.g., "G, A, B...").
- Pick up your bass and read through the exercise with the click. Do your best to stay with the tempo.
- As you get more comfortable with the click, gradually speed up the tempo.

THE CLASSIC RHYTHM

The **dotted quarter/eighth note** combination (the "classic rhythm") is one of the most common in bass playing. Remember, a dot adds one half the value of whatever note it sits next to. A *dotted quarter note* equals the value of three eighth notes (♩. = ♩ + ♪). The classic rhythm is commonly used in one of two variations, and can be applied to many styles of music.

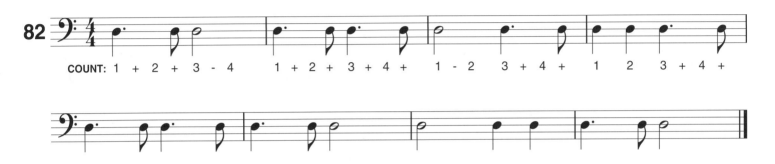

Practice the rhythm slowly, and count out loud. Once familiar with it, use a metronome clicking quarter notes.

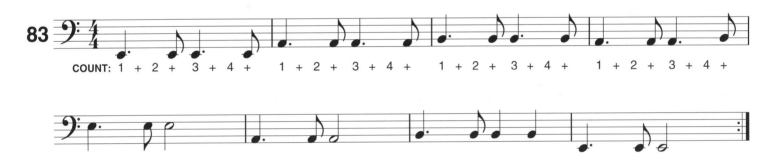

Now use the classic rhythm with a moving line. Keep counting through the second line.

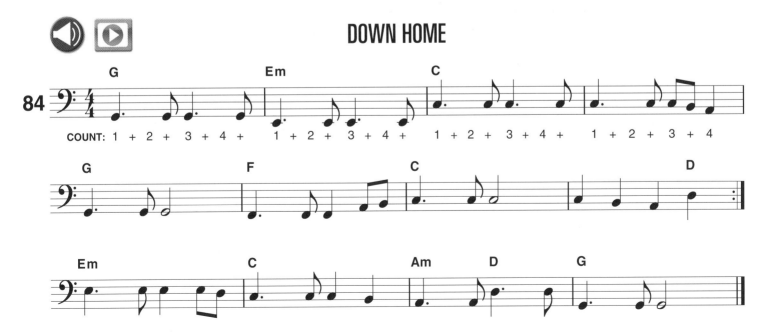

Now we start to add occasional eighth notes to the line. They add interest but keep the feel consistent.

DOWN HOME

This one uses the classic rhythm in a bluesy, R&B style.

RAITT ON

Playing the classic rhythm with octaves is tricky at first. Practice your string crossing. Notice how the 1st ending line leads back to the top, and the 2nd ending line leads to the B section. Make sure to follow the form correctly.

MINOR'S TALE

A CLASSIC VARIATION

Sometimes the classic rhythm is played short: a quarter note followed by an eighth rest, with an eighth note on the upbeat. The space from the rest leaves room for the snare drum to hit on beats 2 and 4, giving the music a tight feel. To create the rest, simply mute the quarter note—either by lifting off the note with the left hand, or placing your plucking finger on the string.

When you get comfortable with this, use the metronome with a quarter-note click. Listen for the space left by the rest.

87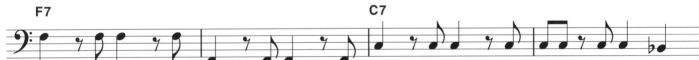

Here is a blues with the shortened classic rhythm.

CLASSIC BLUES

88

PETTY THIEF

89

41

THIRD POSITION

ON THE G STRING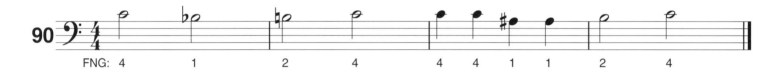

Place your first finger at the 3rd fret. This is **3rd position**. On the G string, this introduces one new note, high C at the 5th fret.

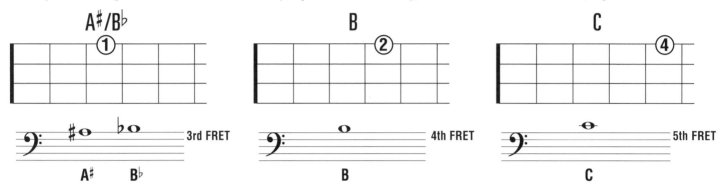

These are all the notes in 3rd position on the G string, starting with the high C.

90

FNG: 4   1   2   4   4   4   1   1   2   4

This example uses the open G string. Do not shift; keep the hand in 3rd position, and simply play the open string.

91

FNG: 4   4   4   1   0   4 0 4 4 1   0   4   2   1   0

If you're playing in 1st or 2nd position, it will be necessary to shift up to the high C. Shifts are indicated with "–".

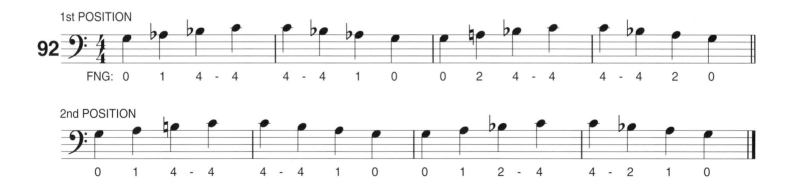

1st POSITION

92

FNG: 0   1   4 – 4   4 – 4   1   0   0   2   4 – 4   4 – 4   2   0

2nd POSITION

0   1   4 – 4   4 – 4   1   0   0   1   2 – 4   4 – 2   1   0

42

ON THE D STRING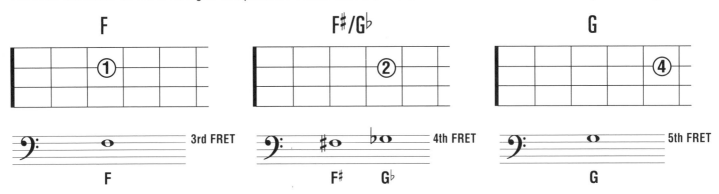

Here are the notes on the D string in 3rd position. Notice that G at the 5th fret is the same note as the open G string.

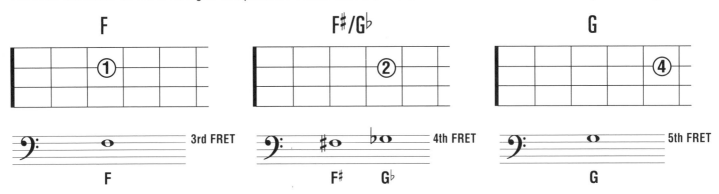

This crosses between the G and D strings in 3rd position.

3RD WATCH

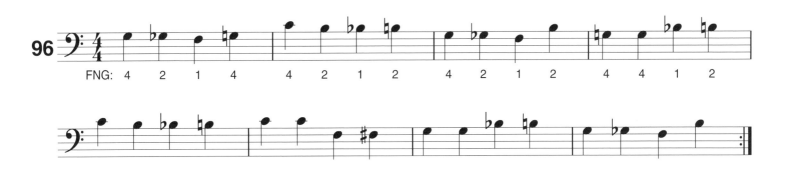

ON THE A STRING

Here are the notes on the A string in 3rd position. The 5th fret is D, the same note as the open D string.

NEW OCTAVE: In 3rd position, we can play an octave on C.

FLYING LEAP

ON THE E STRING ▶

Here are the notes on the E string in 3rd position. The 5th fret is A, the same note as the open A string.

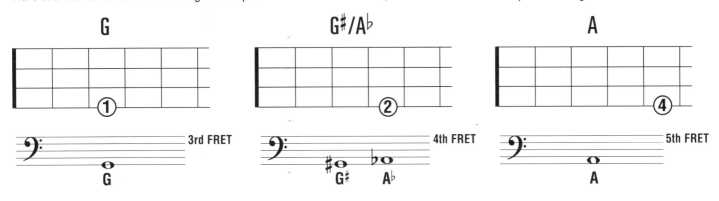

NEW OCTAVE: In 3rd position, we can play an octave on G.

This uses the new octaves on G and C. They are on the same fret, just one string apart.

🔊 ▶   0 AND 3

SHIFTING THROUGH THE POSITIONS ▶️

It is not uncommon to play a song in all three positions. Sometimes you have to shift the octave shape up and down.

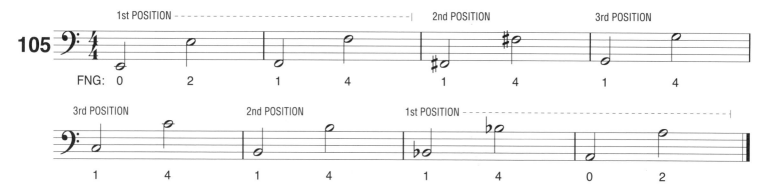

Sometimes it's better to shift to 3rd position for the sake of keeping groups of notes together on the fingerboard.

🔊 ▶️

SHIFTY

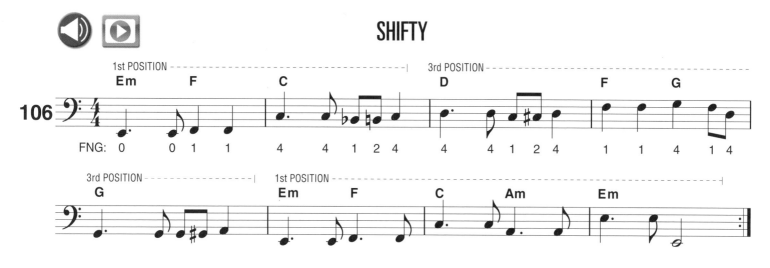

This jazz line shifts freely between 1st, 2nd, and 3rd positions. Brackets indicate what notes are in the same position. The shifts come after an open string, giving you a chance to change positions. Shift marks are placed in the fingering numbers.

🔊

SHIFT-CRAZY BLUES

These examples change positions a few times. See if you can find the best way to play them on your own.

STONES-Y

Additional BONUS CONTENT can be found at **www.halleonard.com/mylibrary** website using the unique code found on page 1!

47

HAL LEONARD
BASS METHOD

METHOD BOOKS

by Ed Friedland

BOOK 1 - 2ND EDITION

Book 1 teaches: tuning; playing position; musical symbols; notes within the first five frets; common bass lines, patterns and rhythms; rhythms through eighth notes; playing tips and techniques; more than 100 great songs, riffs and examples; and more! The audio includes 44 full-band tracks for demonstration or play-along.
00695067 Book Only..............................$9.99
00695068 Book/Online Audio.............................$14.99
01100122 Deluxe - Book/Online Audio/Video $19.99

BOOK 2 - 2ND EDITION

Book 2 continues where Book 1 left off and teaches: the box shape; moveable boxes; notes in fifth position; major and minor scales; the classic blues line; the shuffle rhythm; tablature; and more!
00695069 Book Only..............................$9.99
00695070 Book/Online Audio.............................$14.99

BOOK 3 - 2ND EDITION

With the third book, progressing students will learn more great songs, riffs and examples; sixteenth notes; playing off chord symbols; slap and pop techniques; hammer-ons and pull-offs; playing different styles and grooves; and more.
00695071 Book Only..............................$9.99
00695072 Book/Online Audio.............................$14.99

COMPOSITE - 2ND EDITION

This money-saving edition contains Books 1, 2 and 3.
00695073 Book Only..............................$19.99
00695074 Book/Online Audio.............................$27.99

DVD

Play your favorite songs in no time with this DVD! Covers: tuning, notes in first through third position, rhythms through eighth notes, fingerstyle and pick playing, 4/4 and 3/4 time, and more! Includes 6 full songs and on-screen music notation. 68 minutes.
00695849 DVD $19.95

BASS FOR KIDS

by Chad Johnson

Bass for Kids is a fun, easy course that teaches children to play bass guitar faster than ever before. Popular songs such as "Crazy Train," "Every Breath You Take," "A Hard Day's Night" and "Wild Thing" keep kids motivated, and the clean, simple page layouts ensure their attention remains focused on one concept at a time.
00696449 Book/Online Audio $14.99

REFERENCE BOOKS

BASS SCALE FINDER

by Chad Johnson

Learn to use the entire fretboard with the *Bass Scale Finder*. This book contains over 1,300 scale diagrams for the most important 17 scale types.
00695781 6" x 9" Edition.....................$9.99
00695778 9" x 12" Edition...................$10.99

BASS ARPEGGIO FINDER

by Chad Johnson

This extensive reference guide lays out over 1,300 arpeggio shapes. 28 different qualities are covered for each key, and each quality is presented in four different shapes.
00695817 6" x 9" Edition.....................$9.99
00695816 9" x 12" Edition...................$9.99

MUSIC THEORY FOR BASSISTS

by Sean Malone

Acclaimed bassist and composer Sean Malone will explain the written language of music, using easy-to-understand terms and concepts, diagrams, and much more. The audio provides 96 tracks of examples, demonstrations, and play-alongs.
00695756 Book/Online Audio $19.99

STYLE BOOKS

BASS LICKS

by Ed Friedland

This comprehensive supplement to any bass method will help students learn over 200 great bass licks, lines and grooves in many rhythmic styles. *Bass Licks* illustrates how simple melodic patterns can become the springboard for group improvisation or the foundation of a song.
00696035 Book/Online Audio $15.99

BASS LINES

by Matt Scharfglass

500 expertly written bass lines, riffs and fills in a wide variety of musical genres are included in this comprehensive collection to help players expand their bass vocabulary. The examples cover many tempos, keys and feels, and include easy bass lines for beginners on up to advanced riffs for more experienced bassists.
00148194 Book/Online Audio $22.99

BLUES BASS

by Ed Friedland

Learn to play studying the songs of B.B. King, Stevie Ray Vaughan, Muddy Waters, Albert King, the Allman Brothers, T-Bone Walker, and many more. Learn riffs from blues classics including: Born Under a Bad Sign • Hideaway • Hoochie Coochie Man • Killing Floor • Pride and Joy • Sweet Home Chicago • The Thrill Is Gone • and more.
00695870 Book/Online Audio $17.99

COUNTRY BASS

by Glenn Letsch

21 songs, including: Act Naturally • Boot Scootin' Boogie • Crazy • Honky Tonk Man • Love You Out Loud • Luckenbach, Texas (Back to the Basics of Love) • No One Else on Earth • Ring of Fire • Southern Nights • Streets of Bakersfield • Whose Bed Have Your Boots Been Under? • and more.
00695928 Book/Online Audio $22.99

FRETLESS BASS

by Chris Kringel

18 songs, including: Bad Love • Continuum • Even Flow • Everytime You Go Away • Hocus Pocus • I Could Die for You • Jelly Roll • King of Pain • Kiss of Life • Lady in Red • Tears in Heaven • Very Early • What I Am • White Room • more.
00695850...$22.99

FUNK BASS

by Chris Kringel

This is your complete guide to learning the basics of grooving and soloing funk bass. Songs include: Can't Stop • I'll Take You There • Let's Groove • Stay • What Is Hip • and more.
00695792 Book/Online Audio..............................$22.99

R&B BASS

by Glenn Letsch

This book/audio pack uses actual classic R&B, Motown, soul and funk songs to teach you how to groove in the style of James Jamerson, Bootsy Collins, Bob Babbitt, and many others. The 19 songs include: For Once in My Life • Knock on Wood • Mustang Sally • Respect • Soul Man • Stand by Me • and more.
00695823 Book/Online Audio $19.99

ROCK BASS

by Sean Malone

This book/audio pack uses songs from a myriad of rock genres to teach the key elements of rock bass. Includes: Another One Bites the Dust • Beast of Burden • Money • Roxanne • Smells like Teen Spirit • and more.
00695801 Book/Online Audio..............................$22.99

SUPPLEMENTARY SONGBOOKS

These great songbooks correlate with Books 1-3 of the *Hal Leonard Bass Method*, giving students great songs to play while they're still learning! The audio tracks include great accompaniment and demo tracks.

EASY POP BASS LINES

20 great songs that students in Book 1 can master. Includes: Come as You Are • Crossfire • Great Balls of Fire • Imagine • Surfin' U.S.A. • Takin' Care of Business • Wild Thing • and more.
00695809 Book/Online Audio..............................$16.99

MORE EASY POP BASS LINES

20 great songs for Level 2 students. Includes: Bad, Bad Leroy Brown • Crazy Train • I Heard It Through the Grapevine • My Generation • Pride and Joy • Ramblin' Man • Summer of '69 • and more.
00695819 Book Only...$14.99
00695818 Book/Online Audio..............................$16.99

EVEN MORE EASY POP BASS LINES

20 great songs for Level 3 students, including: ABC • Another One Bites the Dust • Brick House • Come Together • Higher Ground • Iron Man • The Joker • Sweet Emotion • Under Pressure • more.
00695821 Book...$14.99
00695820 Book/Online Audio..............................$16.99

Visit Hal Leonard online at
www.halleonard.com